Wild Predators!

Sea Hunters:
Dolphins, Whales, and Seals

Heinemann Library
Chicago, Illinois

Andrew Solway

Design: David Poole and Calcium
Illustrations: Geoff Ward
Picture Research: Maria Joannou and Catherine
  Bevan
Production: Camilla Smith

Originated by Ambassador Litho Ltd.
Printed and bound in China by
South China Printing Company.

09 08 07 06 05
10 9 8 7 6 5 4 3 2 1

**Library of Congress Cataloging-in-
Publication Data**
Solway, Andrew.
  Sea hunters : dolphins, whales, and seals /
Andrew Solway.-- 1st ed.
     p. cm. -- (Wild predators)
  Includes bibliographical references (p.   ).
  ISBN 1-4034-6569-X (hc) -- ISBN 1-4034-
6575-4 (pb)
  1. Cetacea--Juvenile literature. 2. Seals
(Animals)--Juvenile literature. I. Title. II. Series.
  QL737.C4S58 2005
  599.5'153--dc22

                                    2004018664

Acknowledgments
The author and publisher are grateful to the
following for permission to reproduce copyright
material:
Arctic Photo p. **15 top**; Ardea pp. **5 top**
(Francois Gohier), **7 top** (Valerie & Ron Taylor),
7 bottom (P Morris), **14** (Don Hadden FPSNZ),
17 (Gohier), **18** (Gohier), **19 top** (Gohier), **23**
(Augusto Leandro Stanzani), **27 top** (Gohier), **28**
(Gohier), **30** (Gohier), **33** (Gohier), **37 top** (Doc
White), **40** (Gohier), **43 top** (Ron & Valerie
Taylor); Corbis pp. **43 bottom** (Bettmann), **27
bottom** (Brandon D. Cole); FLPA pp. **5 bottom**
(Minden Pictures), **6** (Silvestris), **8** (Minden
Pictures), **9 bottom** (Gerard Lacz), **10** (Lacz), **12**
(Minden Pictures), **15 bottom** (Minden Pictures),
16 (Sunset), **19 bottom** (Lacz), **21** (Lacz), **22**
(Minden Pictures), **24** (Minden Pictures), **25**
(E Pitman/Earthviews), **31** (Lacz), **34** (Minden
Pictures), **36** (Lacz), **37 bottom** (Minden
Pictures), **42** (Minden Pictures); Natural History
Museum p. **4**; Naturepl pp. **32** (Florian Graner);
NHPA pp. **26** (Patrick Fagot), **38** (Todd Pusser);
Oxford Scientific Films pp. **9 top** (Konrad
Wothe), **13** (Howard Hall), **29** (David Fleetham);
Sea Pics pp. **39**, **41**; Still Pictures p. **35**.

Cover photograph of a leopard seal (*Hydrurga
leptany*) with Adelie penguin prey underwater,
Antartica, reproduced with permission of
Naturepl/Doug Allan.

The publisher would like to thank Dr Randall
Wells of the Chicago Zoological Society and the
Center for Marine Mammal and Sea Turtle
Research at the Mote Marine Laboratory for his
assistance in the preparation of this book.

Every effort has been made to contact copyright
holders of any material reproduced in this book.
Any omissions will be rectified in subsequent
printings if notice is given to the publisher.

Contents

Mammals at Sea

Suppose you could go back in time 50 million years, to the banks of a river in Pakistan. If you were lucky, you might see a wolf-sized creature called *Pakicetus* diving for fish in the water. The animal looks like a long-legged otter with a pointed snout. It may not seem like it, but *Pakicetus* is an ancestor of today's whales.

Ten million years later, the descendants of animals like *Pakicetus* had adapted completely to life in water. Their back legs disappeared and were replaced by a broad tail. Their front legs became fins, and their hair mostly disappeared and was replaced by a thick layer of fat (blubber). By about 40 million years ago, whale-like animals up to 60 feet (18 meters) long were swimming in the world's oceans.

Modern whales include some of the largest, most intelligent predators on Earth. Sea hunters such as killer whales compete successfully with sharks and other top fish predators.

Whales and dolphins

There are about 85 different species in the whale family, including 42 species of dolphins and porpoises. Whales, dolphins, and porpoises are together known as cetaceans. Cetaceans are completely adapted to life in the sea. They even give birth in the water.

Most whales are hunters, but the largest, like the massive blue whale, eat tiny animals such as krill.

Scientists have reconstructed what *Pakicetus* might have looked like from fossil bones found in Pakistan.

Biggest ever

The blue whale may be the biggest animal that ever lived, either on land or in the sea. Blue whales can grow to a length of 88 feet (27 meters), and can weigh 150 tons. The heart of a blue whale is as big as a car!

Although they spend their whole lives in water and can dive to great depths, whales cannot breathe underwater like fish. They must regularly come to the surface for air.

Other sea mammals

Whales are not the only mammals that have adapted to life in the ocean. Two other groups of animals, the sirenians and the pinnipeds, spend all or most of their lives at sea.

There are about 34 different species of pinniped, including seals, sea lions, and walruses. Most are predators, although some gather shellfish and other small prey rather than hunting their food. Pinnipeds spend most of their lives at sea, but they do come onto land to breed and to molt. Their closest relatives on land are animals such as bears, dogs, and cats.

There are just four sirenian species—the dugong and three species of manatee. All four sirenians eat only plants and never come onto land. They are sometimes known as sea cows.

The teeth of sea mammals are usually triangular and pointed, as this is the best shape for catching fish.

The Seal Family

It is summer, and a group of walruses are resting on an island in the northern Pacific Ocean. One walrus leaves the group and dives to the shallow seabed, searching for food. It feels around in the mud with its walrus mustache of whiskers until it finds a shellfish. Then it digs it out and sucks the soft body out of the shell.

All seals are meat eaters, but not all are true predators that hunt large prey. Walruses, for instance, gather shellfish and other small animals from the seabed.

Most seals are not fussy eaters—they will take whatever food they can catch. A few species catch warm-blooded prey such as penguins, and sometimes even other seals.

Living in cold seas

Many seals live in the cold oceans around the North and South Poles. Staying warm in such cold water is a major problem for warm-blooded animals. An animal loses heat much faster in water than it does in air. A thick blanket of blubber just beneath the skin helps keep the seal warm. As well as providing insulation, the blubber does other jobs. It stores energy for when food is scarce, and it helps the seal float. Blubber also makes the seal's body more streamlined.

Changes for sea life

Pinnipeds have had to adapt in many ways to cope with life at sea. Their front and back legs have become flippers, and their bodies have become streamlined to move easily through the water. Their eyes can focus as well underwater as on land, and their hearing is adapted to work well underwater.

Sea lions can run quite fast on land. They can also climb.

True seals and fur seals

There are three main groups of pinnipeds—true seals, eared seals (sea lions and fur seals), and walruses. As their name suggests, eared seals have small ears, while true seals have an ear opening, but no external ear.

True seals swim using their hind (back) flippers. On land these hind flippers are of little use, and the seals must crawl on their belly. Eared seals are more agile on land. They use their front flippers for swimming, and on land they turn their hind flippers around and use them like feet.

Walruses

Walruses are different from both eared and true seals. Both male and female walruses have large tusks and whiskers on their nose that look like a mustache. Like true seals, walruses have no ears, but like eared seals they can turn their hind flippers around to walk on land.

Squid are a main food for many seals. They are mollusks, like snails and slugs. There are many different squid species. These arrow squid travel in large schools.

California Sea Lion

A group of California sea lions has gathered offshore to rest and to play after feeding. One group floats together in a closely packed raft. Another group of younger sea lions are following one after another. When the leader leaps out of the water, the others follow. Another group of sea lions is surfing on the waves.

California sea lions are eared seals. They live along the west coast of North America, and on the Galapagos Islands in the Pacific Ocean. There are fourteen species of eared seals—five sea lion species and nine species of fur seals. Fur seals are similar to sea lions, but they have a dense layer of fur that helps keep them warm.

Adaptable hunters

Like most seals, California sea lions will eat whatever prey is available. They hunt for squid, and for fish, such as mackerel, sardines, and salmon.

California sea lions are fast, acrobatic swimmers. Their speed and agility enable them to catch fast-swimming fish. Although they usually hunt alone, California sea lions will feed in groups if there are large schools of fish or squid. By working together, the seals can stop the fish from escaping while they feed.

California sea lions can swim at speeds of up to 25 miles (40 kilometers) per hour. They usually feed in shallow water but can dive to 490 feet (150 meters) below.

California sea lions are playful and social animals. They often rest and hang out together in groups after feeding.

Fighting on the beaches

Like other eared seals, California sea lions come onto land once a year to mate and give birth. They breed only on a few islands that are out of reach of predators.

Male California sea lions are much bigger than females.
This is because they fight each other for the chance to mate with females.
During the breeding season, each male tries to claim part of a breeding beach.
The males will mate with all the females on their stretch of beach.

Females arrive at the breeding beaches ready to give birth. A short time after producing pups and beginning to suckle, the females mate with the males. The young resulting from these matings will not be born until the following year.

Bringing up pups

Female California sea lions suckle their pups for several months, alternating between feeding themselves in the sea and feeding their pups. After four or five months a pup is able to follow its mother into the sea.

With other eared seals, the males are also much bigger than the females. Male northern fur seals can be twice as long and four times as heavy as females.

Seal sleep

Sea lions and seals sleep underwater, but they must continue to breathe while asleep. They do this by lying just beneath the surface and poking their noses out of the water so they can breathe every few minutes without waking up.

Harp Seal

The water in which the harp seal swims looks pitch black to human eyes, but the seal can see in the very dim light. Swimming on its back, it spots the silvery flashes of a school of small fish called capelin and feels the vibrations of their movement. Shooting upward, the seal darts right and left, catching several fish before the school scatters.

Harp seals are medium-sized true seals, about 71 inches (180 centimeters) long, that live in the sea and on the pack ice off the coasts of Canada, Greenland, and Russia. Adult harp seals feed mostly on fish and on small, shrimp-like crustaceans.

Following the food

Harp seals spend most of their lives traveling. Female harp seals give birth in early spring in breeding areas such as the Gulf of St. Lawrence in Canada. In late spring the seals head north to summer feeding grounds rich in fish. In the autumn they move south again as the seas freeze over.

For most of the year, harp seals travel and hunt together in groups. A single seal feeding on a school of fish finds it hard to pick out a single fish among the dense crowd. However, when several seals feed together they can scatter the school and pick off individual fish.

Harp seals are also known as saddlebacks. Both names come from the large patches of dark fur on the seals' backs, which can be harp-shaped or can look like a saddle.

Killed for fur

From the 18th to the 20th centuries, harp seals were killed in large numbers for their fur and fat. Thousands of whitecoats were killed. In the 1980s the killing of whitecoats was banned, but hundreds of thousands of raggedy-jackets are still killed each year for their fur.

Whitecoats and raggedy-jackets

In the early spring, thousands of female harp seals gather at breeding sites on the ice and give birth to their pups. Each female produces just one pup.

The pups are small and thin at first, with a coat of white, woolly fur. Whitecoats, as they are known, begin to feed as soon as they are born. The mother seal's milk is extremely rich, and the whitecoats grow quickly. In just ten or twelve days they triple in weight.

When the pups are two weeks old, their white coat begins to fall out in tufts, revealing a spotted gray coat beneath. Pups at this stage are called raggedy-jackets. Soon after this, the seal mothers leave to head north. The pups are left stranded on the ice, but eventually hunger forces them into the water, where they feed on small crustaceans.

Although whitecoats are now protected, over 200,000 harp seal pups are killed each year in Canada alone.

Southern Elephant Seal

On an island near the Antarctic, the beach is crowded with elephant seals. The noise is tremendous! Hungry pups squawk and yelp for their mothers, and their mothers reply with growling calls. Bull elephant seals warn each other off with short, rumbling roars. One pair of bulls begins a full-blown fight, roaring, pushing against each other, and gnashing their teeth.

Southern elephant seals are the biggest of all seals. Males can grow to longer than twenty feet (six meters) and weigh four tons. Females are much smaller—they grow to about 8 feet (2.5 meters) and weigh up to 1,800 pounds (800 kilograms). Full-grown males have a small trunk that gives the seals their name.

Southern elephant seals are true seals. They live in the Southern Ocean around Antarctica. Twice each year they climb onto isolated beaches—once to breed and raise pups, and once to molt.

Life at sea

At sea, elephant seals travel vast distances. Scientists believe that some seals can cover about 10,000 miles (16,000 kilometers) each year.

The entire time they are at sea, elephant seals are diving to feed. Sea elephants mainly hunt at depths of up to 2,300 feet (700 meters) or more. Their main prey are squid and large fish, including small sharks. Occasionally they also catch seabirds and penguins.

Elephant seals are the champion divers among seals. They have been recorded diving to maximum depths of 5,577 feet (1,700 meters) and staying underwater for 2 hours.

Adapted for diving

Both seals and whales have adapted in many ways for making long dives. They do not have particularly large lungs, but their blood and their muscles are extremely good at storing oxygen. When elephant seals dive, their heart rate slows to just a few beats per minute. Parts of the body that are not needed for diving shut down.

A tough fight to breed

For male elephant seals, the breeding season is a tough time. Males arrive at the breeding beaches weeks before the females. They fight each other for the chance to mate with females. When the females arrive, successful males mate with 50 or more females, but most males do not mate at all.

In their fights, the males inflate their trunks, rear up, push against each other, and bite with their large canine (front) teeth.

Abandoned early

Elephant seal females give birth to a single pup. At birth the pup has black, curly fur. Seal pups grow very fast on their rich diet of mother's milk. The pups feed for only 23 days, after which their mothers head back to sea, abandoning the pups. The pups stay on shore until hunger drives them into the water.

Elephant seals take many years to grow. Females begin to breed at three or four years old, but males rarely get to mate before they are ten years old.

Leopard Seal

In Antarctica, hundreds of penguin chicks stand on the ice edge, ready to swim for the first time. Out of sight under an overhang, a leopard seal surfaces to breathe, then silently dives again. The chicks at last take the plunge and swim frantically out to sea. The leopard seal, lurking below, sees one chick that has lost its way. Gliding up through the water, it grabs the penguin in its fierce jaws.

Of all the seals, leopard seals are the fiercest and most dangerous. They live around the edges of the pack ice in Antarctica.

Warm-blooded killers

Leopard seals are the only seals that regularly hunt warm-blooded prey. They catch sea birds, penguins, and other seals, as well as cold-blooded prey, such as fish, squid, and tiny, shrimp-like animals called krill.

Only the biggest leopard seals catch larger prey such as adult penguins and other seals. They attack most Antarctic seal species, especially the small crabeater seal. Both seals and penguins are good swimmers and are hard to catch. However, leopard seals have enlarged front flippers compared to other true seals, and these give them extra speed and maneuverability.

Leopard seals have a slim body, a spotted coat, and a large head with huge jaws. Female leopard seals are bigger than males. They can grow to nearly 11 feet (3.5 meters) in length.

Leopard seals are one of the top predators in Antarctic seas. They are dangerous even to humans. They have been known to attack people underwater or on the pack ice.

Hunting tactics

Leopard seals hunt alone. They depend on surprise when attacking. They often swim close to the sea bed, where their spotted coat gives them camouflage.

Leopard seals also sometimes hunt on the ice edge. To catch penguins, a leopard seal may lurk just below the surface and look for shadows on the ice above. When it spots a penguin, it will leap out of the water onto the ice, snatch its prey, and drag it back into the water.

Secret pups

Little is known about how leopard seals reproduce, and very few people have ever seen leopard seal pups. During the breeding season, both male and female leopard seals sing. These calls probably helps them find partners for mating. Females probably give birth to a single pup in November (the Antarctic summer). The females suckle the pup for only a short period—about four weeks.

Leopard seal attacks are not always successful. These penguins have escaped by climbing onto the pack ice.

A mixture of weapons

A leopard seal's front teeth are sharp daggers designed to bite and hold large prey. But at the back of its mouth it has teeth that are designed for filtering krill from the water.

Whales

On a boat off the coast of Australia, a group of people is watching whales. Earlier they saw dolphins riding the boat's wake like surfers. Now they have found two adult humpback whales and a calf. As they approach, one of the adults, more than 39 feet (12 meters) long, leaps out of the water and falls back with a tremendous splash.

For hundreds of years people hunted whales for their meat and blubber, but today whale watching is more popular than hunting. The whale family includes killer whales, porpoises, and dolphins.

When they surface to breathe, whales shoot out a cloud of vapor in what is known as a *blow*. Different whale species have different blows. This picture shows a group of killer whales blowing.

At home in the sea

Unlike seals, whales and dolphins spend their whole lives at sea. Seals still have fur on their bodies, but whales have smooth skin and rely on blubber to keep them warm. A seal's flippers are modified legs, but whales have a fish-like tail that moves up and down to steer them through the water.

Saved from drowning

Although they have adapted well to living in water, whales must breathe air. If a whale is hurt and cannot surface to breathe, it will drown. Perhaps for this reason, whales are known to help a companion that is injured by supporting it at the surface. Some species, such as false killer whales and dolphins, will help other kinds of whales or even humans that get into difficulties.

Whales do not breathe through their mouth, but through a blowhole on the top of their head. This means that only the top of their head needs to be above water to allow them to breathe.

A world of sound

Although whales have good vision, their most important sense is hearing. Sound travels much farther in water than in air, and whales use sound to communicate over long distances. The sounds made by a fin whale, for instance, can travel about 500 miles (800 kilometers). Dolphins and other toothed whales (see below) also use sound to navigate their environment and to find prey.

Baleen whales

The whale family can be divided into two main branches—baleen whales and toothed whales. Baleen whales include the biggest whales, such as the blue whale and the fin whale. They do not have teeth, but instead have hard baleen plates in their mouth that they use to strain tiny creatures such as krill from the water.

Toothed whales

There are about 72 different kinds of toothed whales, including 36 different dolphins and 6 types of porpoise (small, dolphin-like whales). Toothed whales are all predators. Most of them hunt fish and squid, but the killer whale also hunts warm-blooded prey.

The mouth of this humpback whale shows the plates of hard baleen that they use to filter small animals out of the water.

Bottlenose Dolphin

At an aquarium the dolphins have been trained to collect garbage in their pool in return for a reward of fish. On one day the pool seems clean, but a dolphin keeps coming up with pieces of garbage. The trainer investigates. He finds that the dolphin has collected an underwater store of garbage and is bringing up pieces for rewards of fish.

Like all dolphins, bottlenose dolphins are acrobatic, playful, and very intelligent. They are the dolphins we see most often in movies or at marine parks.

Impossible speeds

All dolphins are fast and agile swimmers. Some can swim through the water at speeds of up to 31 mph (50 km/h). For many years scientists were puzzled about how dolphins could reach such speeds. Tests using dolphin models suggested that they would need a lot more muscle to swim so fast.

In recent years researchers have discovered that the key to a dolphin's speed is its skin. Tiny ridges on the skin, similar to our fingerprints, follow the path that the water takes as it flows over a dolphin's body. The ridges help water flow more smoothly and reduce drag.

The skin also produces tiny drops of oil that help the dolphin move smoothly through the water.

Bottlenose dolphins usually live near coasts, but some live in the open ocean.

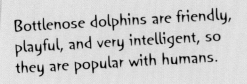

Bottlenose dolphins are friendly, playful, and very intelligent, so they are popular with humans.

Bottlenose dolphins are fairly large dolphins, measuring between 71 to 154 inches (180 and 390 centimeters). Usually males are much bigger than females. In the wild, bottlenose dolphins live in warm or temperate seas around the world.

All kinds of food

Bottlenose dolphins eat all kinds of food, but primarily fish and squid. Some bottlenose dolphins have also learned to follow fishing boats, eating the fish that escape from the nets.

Bottlenose dolphins often hunt alone, but sometimes they hunt in small groups. Most bottlenose dolphins hunt in fairly shallow water, but off the west coast of Africa they dive to depths of about 1,640 feet (500 meters) searching for prey.

When traveling fast, bottlenose dolphins leap out of the water to breathe. Surprisingly, leaping out of the water uses less energy than just rising above the surface.

When hunting, bottlenose dolphins sometimes work together with split-second timing to trap and catch prey.

Hunting methods

Bottlenose dolphins hunt their prey in many different ways. Often they hunt alone or in small groups, and find fish by the sounds the fish produce. Sometimes they use echolocation to help them find schools of fish or other prey, and then work together to trap the fish in a small area. Usually this happens in the open sea, but not always. For instance, off the coast of South Carolina, muddy marshes slope gently to the sea. Small groups of dolphins swim slowly back and forth near a bank of mud, herding fish close to the shore. Then, all together, the dolphins turn and rush at great speeds toward the shore. Their rush creates a wave that sweeps up the fish and strands them on the mud. The dolphins follow the fish, turning on their sides to snap them up.

In the open ocean there are no banks or bays to trap fish, so the dolphins work differently. Larger groups of dolphins swim around and below a school of fish, bunching them together and driving them up to the surface, where they are trapped. The dolphins then take turns feeding while their companions keep the fish together.

Burps, clicks, and whistles

Bottlenose dolphins could not hunt in these ways without being able to communicate with each other. Dolphins use many different sounds to communicate. If you lowered an underwater microphone into the water

Bottlenose echolocation

All toothed whales rely heavily on sound to find their way around and to hunt prey. Sometimes they just listen, or they use a system called echolocation. Dolphins make a fast string of high-pitched clicking sounds, and the echoes of these clicks bounce back from the objects around them. From the echoes the dolphins can tell how far away an object is, something about its shape and size, whether it is moving, and even what it is made of. To investigate an object more thoroughly, bottlenose dolphins can send out a very narrow beam of clicks, to get detailed information from a small area in front of them.

near a group of dolphins, you would hear an incredible variety of sounds—whistles, grunts, clicks, chuckles, squeaks, pops, and burps. Each individual dolphin has a signature whistle that identifies them to other dolphins. Another sound, something like a creaky hinge, is the echolocation sound they sometimes use to explore their environment.

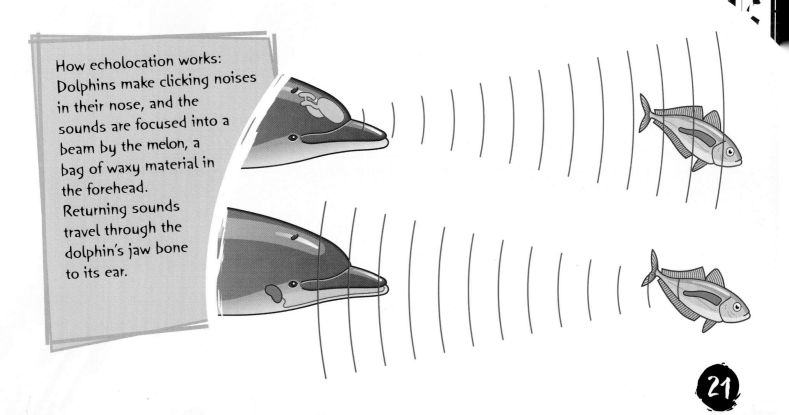

How echolocation works:
Dolphins make clicking noises in their nose, and the sounds are focused into a beam by the melon, a bag of waxy material in the forehead.
Returning sounds travel through the dolphin's jaw bone to its ear.

Having fun

Dolphins are social animals, and seem to enjoy spending time together. After feeding they often gather in groups to socialize. They greet each other by calling, swimming close, and touching each other with their flippers. They also seem to play together—leaping, chasing each other, performing acrobatics, surfing on the waves, or perhaps passing a piece of seaweed from one dolphin to the next.

Researchers think that some of a dolphin's playful activities may have a practical purpose, perhaps in communication or courtship, or to practice skills they need for other parts of life. However, dolphins have such a variety of playful behaviors that it seems likely they are sometimes just having fun.

Mating and young

In dolphin groups, males and females do not pair up for long periods. Males and females may both mate with many different partners. When mating is successful, a single dolphin calf is born about twelve months later. When the calf comes out of its mother, it instinctively swims towards the surface to take its first breath. The mother helps it along, swimming underneath the calf and nudging it upward.

Dolphins often hunt in small groups and then meet up in larger numbers to rest and play together.

Bottlenose dolphin young are born tail first, rather than head first as most mammals are.

Within minutes the calf is able to swim with its mother. The calf stays very close to its mother, swimming right by her side. By swimming so close the calf is less likely to be noticed by predators. It also gets an easy ride when swimming, because it is pulled along in its mother's slipstream.

Dolphin calves develop over a long period. They feed on their mother's milk for up to twelve months, although after a few months they begin to catch their own food. They stay with their mother for three years or more, and are not fully adult until they are at least five years old. Females become adult at five to ten years old, but males do not breed until they are about ten years old.

Hunting dolphins

Many people think dolphins are beautiful, intelligent animals and find the idea of killing them terrible. But every year hundreds of thousands of dolphins are killed. Numbers of some species, such as spotted dolphins, have fallen dramatically.

In a few places dolphins are hunted as food, but many more are killed accidentally. One major cause of death is fishing boats. These boats trail nets and lines, which are sometimes very long with hundreds of hooks, and dolphins get caught in them and die. Dolphins can also swallow pieces of line or hooks. Pollution is another cause of harm to dolphins, because toxic (poisonous) chemicals become concentrated in their bodies.

Spinner Dolphin

Tuna fishers in the Pacific Ocean are on the lookout for dolphins. They spot a group in the distance and turn toward them. At once the dolphins explode into action, churning up the water as they move away in a series of long, low leaps. Then one of the dolphins leaps almost straight up out of the water, spinning like a top as it jumps. The fishermen count six spins before the dolphin crashes back into the sea.

Spinner dolphins get their name from the acrobatic, spinning leaps that they make when traveling. They are small dolphins that are usually found in the open ocean. Spinner dolphins live in warm and temperate oceans. Their size and markings vary in different parts of the world, but their acrobatic leaps make them easy to identify.

No one knows why spinner dolphins leap as they do. They may do it to dislodge suckerfish that attach to their skin.

Dolphins and tuna

Tuna fishers look out for dolphins because spinners, spotted dolphins, and yellowfin tuna are often found together. The dolphins' echolocation system makes them very good at finding prey, such as squid and lantern fish, which are both foods that tuna eat. The tuna follow the dolphins because they lead them to food.

Night feeders

Most dolphins are daytime feeders, but spinners are active at night. Lantern fish, which are one of the spinner's main foods, dive into deep waters during the day, but at night they come closer to the surface to feed, making them easier to hunt.

Half asleep

Dolphins need to be conscious 24 hours a day because they have to breathe every few minutes. If they fell asleep as we do, they would soon drown. So when dolphins sleep, they rest only one half of their brain at a time. The other half stays alert enough to keep the dolphin afloat and breathing.

Like other dolphins, spinners cooperate with each other to trap fish and herd them together. Spinners often make loud noises as they are herding fish, slapping their tails on the surface. These sounds may help with the herding.

Social gatherings

Open ocean dolphins—like spinners, spotted, and common dolphins—gather in large groups of hundreds or even thousands. They meet up to relax, rest, and play. There is safety in numbers, and gathering in large groups gives small dolphins some protection from predators such as sharks.

When they hunt, spinners travel in smaller groups of up to 100. Because they can communicate over long distances, the dolphins can easily find the larger group again after a hunting expedition.

This small group of spinner dolphins travels together in tight formation. Spinners are similar in size to humans— about 6 feet (1.8 meters) long and weighing as much as about 165 pounds (75 kilograms).

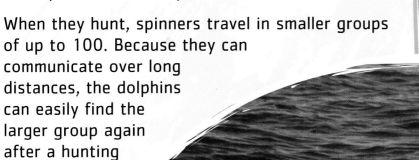

Killer Whale

It is spring in the Antarctic, and the ice is breaking up. On one large chunk of ice a seal is lying asleep. Three killer whales appear in the sea. They circle the ice, but they cannot get at the seal. Then two of the killer whales swim underneath one end of the ice and begin to lift. The ice tilts, and the seal slides off—straight into the waiting jaws of the third whale.

Killer whales are sometimes called orcas, which means "wolves of the sea." They are the top predators in the oceans. They have no natural enemies except for humans. Although they are called whales, killer whales belong to the dolphin family. They are the biggest of the dolphins. Males can reach a length of almost 33 feet (10 meters) and weigh as much as 7 tons, while females can be 23 feet (7 meters) long and weigh 3 tons.

Top hunters

Killer whales are found in all the oceans of the world, although they prefer to live in cooler, shallow waters. They are fast swimmers that can swim at more than 28 mph (45 km/h), but they do not dive very deep and their dives last only a few minutes.

Killer whales are the only cetaceans that feed regularly on large, warm-blooded prey, such as penguins, seals, and even other whales. However, these are not the only animals that killer whales hunt. They also catch many other kinds of prey, including tuna, salmon, herring, sharks, rays, and squid.

Killer whales are black and white, with short, rounded snouts. They have fewer teeth than most dolphins, but their teeth are bigger.

Female killer whales have a curved fin on their backs, but the male's fin is triangular in shape and can be taller than a human. Just behind the fin there is a gray saddle.

Pods for life

Most dolphins live in loose groups that often change, but killer whales live in tight-knit groups, called pods, that they often stay with for life. A pod can have up to 40 whales. It includes adult males and females, calves, and youngsters. Sometimes two or more pods join up for a short time to form large groups of 100 or more killer whales.

The whales in a pod are close relatives. There are brothers and sisters, aunts and uncles, and mothers, but no fathers. Killer whales mate outside their home pod, so the father of a killer whale is always from another pod.

Whale study

Scientists studying killer whales photograph their fins and gray saddles, and use them as a way of identifying individual whales. This has made it possible for researchers to track killer whales over long distances and many years. The fins and saddles of different killer whales are all different.

Hunting methods

Like other dolphins, killer whales are very adaptable hunters. They use different hunting methods depending on their prey and the place they are hunting. Different pods specialize in hunting particular prey.

Many killer whales hunt schooling fish. For instance, several pods of killer whales near Norway work together to hunt herring, which appear every autumn in huge schools. The killers separate a group of several thousand herring and herd the fish into a small volume of water. Rather than chasing individual fish, the killer whales use their tails to stun a whole group with one tremendous swipe.

On the coasts of Argentina, killer whales hunt young fur seals and elephant seals. One pod of killers even attacks seals on the beach. In the autumn, when many young seals are going to sea for the first time, the killer whales leap out of the water and half onto the beach. They grab young seals at the water's edge, then wriggle quickly backwards into the sea.

Catching young sea lions in the surf is tricky for killer whales. They must get high enough up the beach to reach the sea lions, but not so high that they get stuck out of the water.

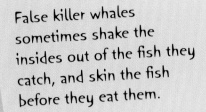

False killer whales sometimes shake the insides out of the fish they catch, and skin the fish before they eat them.

False killers

In the wild, killer whales are sometimes confused with another species called the false killer whale. False killers are slightly smaller than true killers, and they do not have the black and white patterning of a killer whale—they are dark except for their belly. Unlike killer whales, they are often seen in the open ocean.

False killers usually eat squid and large fish, such as bonito, but they sometimes attack small dolphins and porpoises.

The biggest prey

Some killer whales hunt porpoises, other dolphins, and even large baleen whales. Along the west coast of North America, for instance, gray whales migrate north each spring from breeding areas near Mexico to summer feeding grounds in the Arctic. Gray whale mothers and their calves take much longer to travel north, because the calves cannot swim as fast as adult whales.

As the whales travel north, pods of killer whales attack the mother and calf pairs. The killers concentrate on the calf, which is about the same size as they are. The mother is much larger, and could seriously injure a killer whale with her tail. The killers charge in and attack the calf, then retreat out of range of the mother. Again and again they ram into the calf, despite the mother's efforts to protect it. Eventually the killer whales pull the exhausted and injured calf under the water, holding it there until it drowns.

Stay-at-homes and travelers

Researchers studying killer whales on the west coast of North America have found that killer whales there seem to be divided in to two types—residents and transients.

Resident killer whales live together their whole lives in large, stable pods. Since females may live for up to 100 years and males for 50 years, each pod has several generations of whales. Resident killer whale pods are very closely connected. Whales in the pod even breathe in unison. Residents rarely hunt warm-blooded animals— their main prey is fish. Along the West Coast, some pods hunt salmon by trapping them in bays.

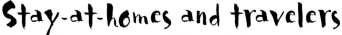

Transients live alone or in pods of up to seven whales. They range much more widely than resident killer whales. Transient killer whales usually hunt mammals, rather than fish. The pods that hunt gray whales in California are transient whales. The same killer whales also hunt sea lions, seals, dolphins, porpoises, and seabirds. Resident and transient killer whales do not seem to breed together, and some biologists think they are separate subspecies.

Killer whales often swim at the surface, sometimes spyhopping (lifting their head above water to look around) and breaching (leaping right out of the water, as in this picture).

Different sounds

Like other dolphins, killer whales use echolocation, and they communicate with clicks, whistles, and honking calls. However, the calls of different pods are not the same. Researchers working with killer whales can sometimes identify different whale pods simply from the sounds they make.

Producing young

Little is known about mating in killer whales, but calves are born thirteen to sixteen months after a successful mating. At birth the calf is already more than 6 feet (2 meters) long and weighs nearly 440 pounds (200 kilograms). Mothers feed their calves on milk for a year to eighteen months.

Once a calf stops drinking its mother's milk, it has to learn to hunt. This can take several years. The young whales have to learn where prey is likely to be found at different times of year, what places are best for hunting, and the different ways of hunting different prey animals. Females are not fully adult until they are ten years old, and males take even longer to mature. Even after they are fully grown, killer whales live and travel with their mothers.

Female killer whales can produce a calf about every three years until they are about 40 years old. After this they help out in the pod by acting as baby-sitters and teachers to young whales.

Young killer whales learn their hunting skills from their mothers and from females that are too old to have calves.

Porpoises

A small group of harbor porpoises is feeding in the channel between two islands. The tide is flowing fast, and a school of herring is swimming close together in the fast-running channel. The porpoises do not hunt in formation like dolphins. They dive at different times, cut across each other's paths, putting on bursts of speed or suddenly changing direction. Their movements are like a very rowdy dance.

Porpoises are similar to dolphins, but there are important differences. Porpoises are usually smaller—the biggest are only 94 inches (240 centimeters) long. They have stocky bodies, and do not have a beak like dolphins. Their teeth are also different. Dolphins have pointed, cone-shaped teeth, but porpoise teeth are shaped like shovels. Like dolphins, porpoises use their teeth to grab prey. Scientists do not know why the teeth of the two groups are different.

Porpoises usually swim alone or in small groups, and they do not leap when they swim fast. Most porpoises are shy and avoid boats or divers.

Similar foods

There are six different species of porpoise. The harbor porpoise, finless porpoise, Burmeister's porpoise, and vaquitas live in shallow waters close to coasts, while the Dall's porpoise and spectacled porpoise are found in the open ocean.

Harbor porpoises are the most widespread porpoises. They are common around coasts throughout the Northern Hemisphere, except in tropical areas.

Dall's porpoises look like small, chubby killer whales. They spew a double jet of spray as they rush through the water.

All porpoises eat schooling fish, squid, and shrimps. Harbor porpoises, which are the most common porpoises, eat mainly herring, mackerel, sardines, and squid. Dall's porpoises are unusual because they feed at night, rather than by day. Like spinner dolphins, they feed on fish, such as lantern fish and hake, which move closer to the surface at night to feed.

Staying warm

Because porpoises are so small, keeping warm is more difficult for them than for larger dolphins and whales. A small animal cools more quickly than a large one, because it has a larger proportion of surface area from which to lose heat.

The plump shape of porpoises helps them to keep warm, and they have a thick insulating layer of blubber. But even so, porpoises cannot keep themselves warm as well as larger whales. They burn more energy to generate heat in their bodies, so they have to eat more food to keep them going.

Hyperactive porpoises

Dall's porpoises live in the North Pacific. They are very active and fast swimmers, reaching top speeds of around 34 mph (55 km/h). They have a giant heart to support their active lifestyle. Unlike other porpoises, Dall's porpoises love to ride the wake from boats.

Amazon River Dolphin

Between January and May, rains swell the rivers of the Amazon Basin, and the waters spread far beyond the riverbanks. Shallow water laps the trunks of the rain forest trees. In the early morning, a long pink shape swims among the trees. It is a river dolphin out looking for breakfast.

Amazon River dolphins live in the rivers of the Amazon Basin. They belong to a group of five dolphin-like whales that live in freshwater. All these river dolphins have a long, thin snout and small eyes. Unlike true dolphins, they have flexible necks and can move their head from side to side.

Blushing pink

When they are born, Amazon river dolphins are a bluish-gray color. As they get older their belly becomes pink, then the pink color slowly spreads upward. Some older adults are bright pink all over. Their snout has a sparse covering of touch-sensitive bristles. Unlike any other whale, a river dolphin has flat-topped chewing teeth at the back of its mouth. Although its eyes are small, an Amazon River dolphin can see well.

Like true dolphins, Amazon River dolphins have a good echolocation system. Researchers have found they can detect something as small as a very thin copper wire.

The most endangered whale

The five river dolphin species are the Yangtze, Ganges, Indus, La Plata, and Amazon River dolphins. The Yangtze River dolphin is the most endangered whale in the world. There are probably fewer than 100 animals left in the wild. Hunting of these dolphins is not allowed, but pollution, illegal hunting, and the greatly increased noise on the river all make it difficult for river dolphins to survive.

Yangtze River dolphins are light gray rather than pink, and they have a short, triangular fin. They hunt at night and in the early morning.

From shrimp to piranhas

Amazon river dolphins hunt many kinds of prey. Most of the fish they eat are 4 to 8 inches (10 to 20 centimeters) long, but they also catch larger fish, including piranhas and armored catfish. Besides fish, river dolphins eat crabs and shrimp, which they nose out of the muddy riverbed. They also eat small turtles. Their chewing teeth are designed for crushing and chewing up turtle shells and the thick skin of armored catfish.

Amazon River dolphins most often hunt alone, along quiet tributaries, or where one river flows into another. These are spots where prey fish tend to gather.

A new generation

Most Amazon river dolphins are born in July to September. Calves are about 31 inches (80 centimeters) long when they are born. The mother feeds her calf on milk for over a year, and the young do not become fully adult until they are at least six years old. River dolphins are thought to live about 30 years.

Beluga and Narwhal

In the freezing waters of the Arctic, a narwhal begins to dive. As it goes under, its heart slows down and blood stops flowing to the skin. Air is slowly pushed out of its lungs and into its throat. The blood and muscles are filled with oxygen and will work for a long time. Now the narwhal has reached 3,280 feet (1,000 meters) below, but it keeps diving. At 4,921 feet (1,500 meters) below, it at last reaches the seabed, and its prey—the halibut.

Belugas and narwhals are closely related whales that are found around the Arctic. Both have thick coverings of blubber to insulate them in the freezing Arctic waters, and both dive deep to find their prey.

White whales

Narwhals are medium-size whales about thirteen to sixteen feet (four to five meters) long. Belugas are a little smaller—about ten to thirteen feet (three or four meters) long. Adult narwhals have a pale belly and a speckled back, while belugas are pure white.

The most remarkable thing about narwhals is the male's tusk. Male narwhals have a spiral tusk that can grow up to ten feet (three meters) long. The tusk is a tooth, which grows through the narwhal's upper lip.

Diving deeper

Belugas and narwhals feed much deeper in the sea than dolphins. Belugas usually feed at depths of 1,640 feet (500 meters) or so, where they hunt schooling fish, crabs, shrimp, and other creatures. Narwhals can feed even deeper, at depths of 4,921 feet (1,500 meters) or more. They eat squid and bottom-dwelling fish such as halibut.

A beluga's bulging forehead is caused by its large melon. This is a tough sac full of oil, which acts as a lens to focus the beluga's echolocating sound beams.

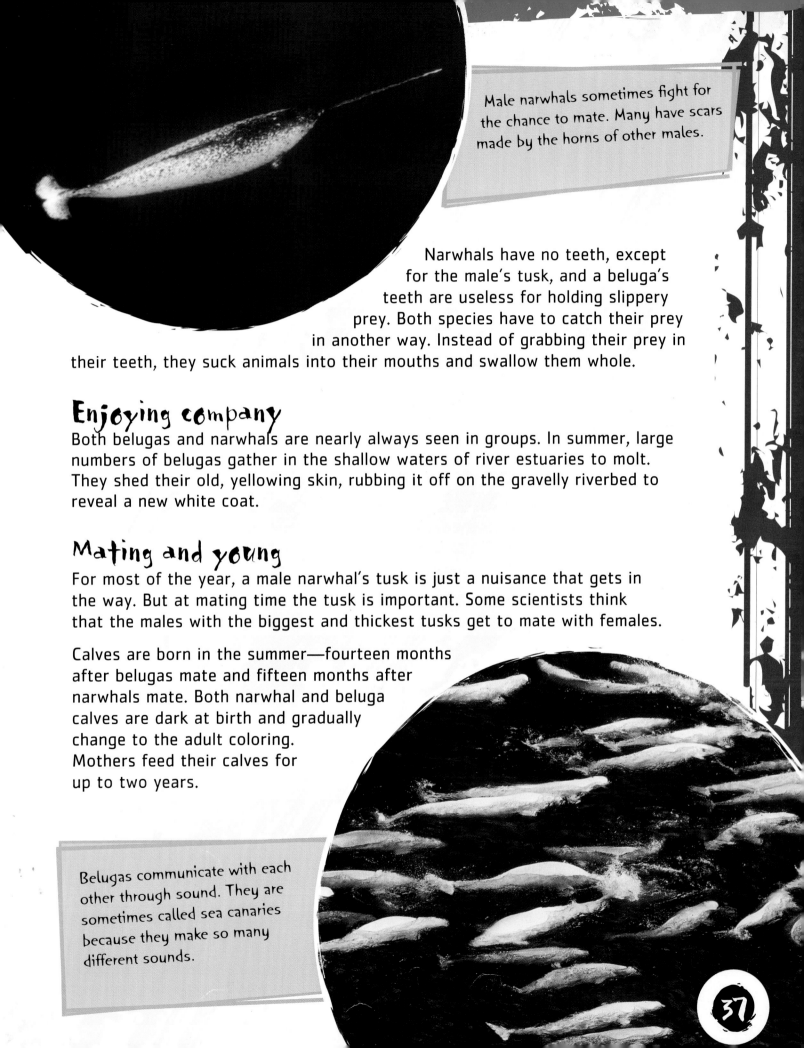

Narwhals have no teeth, except for the male's tusk, and a beluga's teeth are useless for holding slippery prey. Both species have to catch their prey in another way. Instead of grabbing their prey in their teeth, they suck animals into their mouths and swallow them whole.

Enjoying company

Both belugas and narwhals are nearly always seen in groups. In summer, large numbers of belugas gather in the shallow waters of river estuaries to molt. They shed their old, yellowing skin, rubbing it off on the gravelly riverbed to reveal a new white coat.

Mating and young

For most of the year, a male narwhal's tusk is just a nuisance that gets in the way. But at mating time the tusk is important. Some scientists think that the males with the biggest and thickest tusks get to mate with females.

Calves are born in the summer—fourteen months after belugas mate and fifteen months after narwhals mate. Both narwhal and beluga calves are dark at birth and gradually change to the adult coloring. Mothers feed their calves for up to two years.

Belugas communicate with each other through sound. They are sometimes called sea canaries because they make so many different sounds.

Beaked and Bottlenose Whales

In deep water off Scotland, a group of whales is moving north to its summer feeding grounds. A boat appears on the horizon and heads toward them. As the boat gets closer, the noise of its engines seems to excite the whales. They dive repeatedly under the boat and slap their tails on the water. One whale turns on its side and looks up at the boat crew. The tube-like beak and bulging forehead show that it is a northern bottlenose whale.

Beaked whales are a group of about twenty species of deep-diving toothed whales. Most of them are rarely seen and are not very well known. At first glance many beaked whales look like large dolphins. The northern bottlenose whale, for instance, has a bottle nose, or beak, like a dolphin. However, there are several differences. Beaked whales have no crease between the beak and the forehead as dolphins do. Beaked whales are also bigger, and their dorsal (back) fins are smaller and closer to the tail.

Deep sea divers

Beaked whales are deep sea feeders. They are rarely seen in water less than 3,280 feet (1,000 meters) deep. Their main prey are deep sea squid, but they also catch fish, lobsters, crabs, and even starfish.

Many male beaked whales are crisscrossed with scars caused by the tusks of other males.

Strange tusks

The strap-tooth whale has very odd tusks. In an adult male the tusks grow up and over the top part of its beak, stopping the whale from opening its mouth more than one or two inches (a few centimeters). Despite this, males seem to eat prey as big as those eaten by females!

Beaked whales need to be good divers to feed so deep. A normal dive is fifteen or twenty minutes, compared to only four minutes or shorter for most dolphins. Some beaked whales can dive for much longer than this. The northern bottlenose whale, for instance, can dive for 70 minutes to depths of 4,921 feet (1,500 meters) or more.

Tusks and tiny teeth

As in narwhals, females and young beaked whales have only very tiny teeth that do not show through the gums. Males, however, have two or sometimes four tusks, which stick out of the side or the front of their mouth. The tusks seem to be used for fighting rather than for feeding.

Beaked whales probably feed by sucking in prey, in a similar way to belugas and narwhals. All beaked whales have two expandable grooves on their throat. Opening up these grooves sucks water into the mouth, and prey with it.

A few beaked whale species have been seen traveling in groups—usually a male with several females and calves. Scientists believe calves be born about ten to fifteen months after mating.

Sperm Whale

A group of female sperm whales and their calves are under attack. Killer whales first attack a calf, but the adult whales rescue it. The sperm whales face inward in a protective ring, using their tails to keep off the killer whales. One female gets separated, and the killer whales focus their attack on her. Then two other females leave the safety of the protective group and swim to rescue the hurt female.

Sperm whales are the biggest of all the toothed whales. Males can be 59 feet (18 meters) long, while females are 36 feet (11 meters) or shorter. Sperm whales are found throughout the world's oceans, from the Arctic to the Antarctic.

Big head

The most amazing thing about a sperm whale is its enormous square head, which takes up about a third of its length. Most of the head is filled with a huge organ full of a soft, waxy substance called spermaceti. The spermaceti organ is probably used in echolocation, in the same way that other toothed whales use the melon.

Male sperm whales eat some fish, as well as squid. On rare occasions they may catch thirteen-foot (four-meter) sharks.

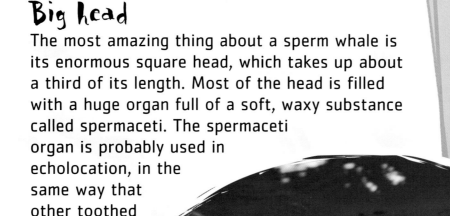

When a sperm whales surfaces after a dive, its first breath is like an explosion. Surfacing after a very deep dive, it may shoot right out of the water, falling back with an incredibly loud smack.

Deep feeders

Although other whales can dive to great depths, sperm whales are the best divers of all. Males have been tracked down to a depth of 7,382 feet (2,250 meters), and can probably reach depths of 9,843 feet (3,000 meters).

The main prey of sperm whales is squid. They eat many different species of deep water squid, including giant and jumbo squid that can be 39 feet (12 meters) long or longer. Most adult sperm whales have round scars caused by the suckers of large squid. These show that the squid often put up a tough fight.

Sperm whales often resurface in the same area where they dived, after staying underwater for 45 minutes or more. Some scientists think that the whales may stay in the same spot deep underwater, lying motionless to surprise prey that come along.

Whale strandings

Many whales, including sperm whales, are found stranded on beaches. Sometimes whole groups of whales get stranded on the same beach. This usually happens when a whale that is ill or injured in some way swims into shallow water to rest. If the water becomes too shallow, the whale gets stuck and cannot swim into deeper water. Mass strandings sometimes happen when a sick or injured whale becomes stranded, and then other whales then get stranded trying to help it.

Separate lives

Male and female sperm whales live very different lives. Females spend their entire lives in warm waters. They spend winter in the Tropics, then move north to temperate seas in summer. Adult males travel much farther in the summer, to the edges of the Arctic and Antarctic ice. In the autumn they move into warmer waters again, where they spend the winter.

Female sperm whales spend several hours each day resting and socializing at the surface. They communicate using a range of click sounds.

Free baby-sitting

Female sperm whales live together in groups of about twelve adults plus their calves. The advantage of group living seems to be free baby-sitting. Sperm whale calves cannot dive as well as adults, so they cannot follow their mothers when they hunt. A single female would have to leave her calf at the surface while she fed, and they would be vulnerable to killer whales or sharks. In a group, the females can dive at different times and always leave adults to guard the young.

Moby Dick

Probably the best known book about whales is Moby Dick, the story of a whaling ship whose captain is obsessed with catching a large white sperm whale called Moby Dick.

Between the 1700s and the 1980s, fleets of whaling ships cruised the world's oceans. They killed millions of whales for oil, blubber, and meat. Today the numbers of all the large whale species are severely reduced.

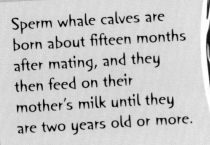

Sperm whale calves are born about fifteen months after mating, and they then feed on their mother's milk until they are two years old or more.

Male sperm whales lead very different lives. At about six years old they leave the female groups and get together with other males of a similar age. As they get older, the males gradually split up, living in smaller and smaller groups. As adults, they spend most of their time alone.

Mating and young

Adult male sperm whales travel to tropical seas each year to meet up with females. The males stay on the move, traveling from one group of females to another, looking for those who are able to mate. In any one year, only a few females can mate, because the process of bringing up young takes four years or more.

Males looking for mates avoid one other as much as possible, but they do sometimes meet and fight. Older males often have scars from the teeth of other males.

Sperm whales were hunted mainly for their spermaceti. This was at first used to make fine candles, then later as an oil for watches and other delicate instruments.

Classification Chart

Scientists classify living things (sort them into groups) by comparing their similarities and differences. A species is a group of animals or plants that are all similar and can breed together to produce young. Similar species are organized into a larger group called a genus (plural genera). Similar genera are grouped into families and so on through bigger and bigger groupings—classes, orders, phyla, and kingdoms.

Seals, whales, dolphins, and porpoises are mammals—they belong to the class Mammalia. Seals are in the order Pinnipedia (pinnipeds), while whales, dolphins, and porpoises are toothed whales (Odontoceti).

Pinnipeds: 33 species in 21 genera

Family	Number of Genera	Number of species	Examples
eared seals (Otariidae) fur seals sea lions	2 5	9 5	northern fur seal California sea lion
walrus (Odobenidae)	1	1	walrus
true seals (Phocidae)	13	18	harp seal, elephant seal, leopard seal

Toothed whales (Odontoceti): 58 species in 48 genera

Family	Number of Genera	Number of species	Examples
River dolphins	4	5	Amazon River dolphin
Dolphins (Delphinidae)	17	36	bottlenose dolphin, spinner dolphin, killer whale
Porpoises (Phocoenidae)	3	6	harbor porpoise, Dall's porpoise
Beluga and narwhal (Monodontidae)	2	2	beluga, narwhal
sperm whale (Physeteridae)	1	1	sperm whale
pygmy sperm whales (Kogiidae)	1	2	dwarf sperm whale, pygmy sperm whale
beaked whales (Ziphiidae)	20	6	northern bottlenose whale

Where Sea Hunters Live

1. Where the seals in this book live

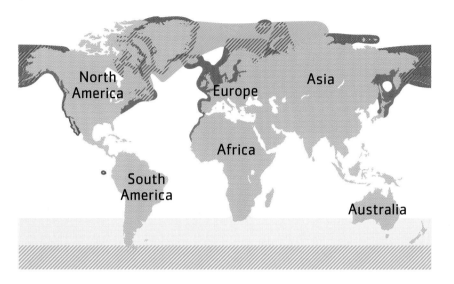

North America
Europe
Asia
Africa
South America
Australia

Key
- California/ Galapagos sea lion
- Harp seal
- Leopard seal
- Harbor porpoise
- Southern elephant seal
- Walrus

2. Where whales and dolphins live

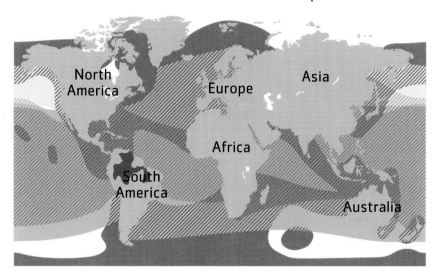

North America
Europe
Asia
Africa
South America
Australia

Key
- Amazon River dolphin
- Bottlenose dolphin
- Spinner dolphin
- Dall's porpoise
- Killer whale

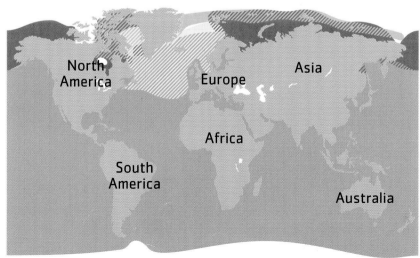

North America
Europe
Asia
Africa
South America
Australia

Key
- Beluga whale
- Narwhal
- Northern bottlenose whale
- Sperm whale

N
W — E
S

Glossary

adapted way that a living thing has changed to fit in with its environment

baleen large, hard plates in a whale's mouth that are used to filter food from seawater

blubber layer of fat beneath the skin in whales, dolphins, seals, and other marine mammals

breed mate and produce young

camouflage coloring and markings on an animal that help it blend in with its environment

cetacean whale, dolphin, or porpoise

class group of closely related families of living things

classify sort into groups

crustacean animal with a hard outer skeleton, such as a crab, lobster, or shrimp

descendant living thing alive today that is directly related to something living in the past

drag force that slows objects down as they move through air or water

echolocation way to locate distant objects using sound waves

family group of closely related genera of living things

fossil remains of an organism that have been preserved in the earth

genus (plural genera) group of species of living things that are closely related

insulation layer of material that stops heat from passing through it

krill small, shrimp-like animals that live in the ocean

maneuverable able to change direction easily

mate when a male and a female animal come together to produce young

melon bag of waxy material in the forehead of dolphins and some other whales that focuses sound

molt lose a layer of old skin

pack ice huge pieces of floating ice packed together in the Arctic and Antarctic oceans

pinniped seal, sea lion, or walrus

predator animal that hunts and eats other animals

prey animal that is hunted by other animals

saddle differently colored skin or hair on an animal's back

schooling fish fish that swim and feed together in large groups

sirenian large mammal that lives in water and feeds on sea grass

slipstream area close to an object moving through air or water

species group of animals that are similar and can breed together to produce healthy offspring

streamlined having a smooth shape to slip easily through water or air

subspecies population of living things within a species that is different from other populations, but not different enough to be a separate species

suckle drink mother's milk

temperate place with a climate that has warm summers and cool winters

transient never staying long in one place

Tropics/tropical land close to the equator where the weather is warm all year

vibration shaking

warm-blooded animal that can keep its body temperature constant even when the environment is colder or hotter

yellowfin tuna kind of large, fast-swimming fish

Further Reading

Baldwin, Carol. *Sea Creatures: Sharks*. Chicago: Heinemann Library, 2003.

Spilsbury, Louise and Richard. *Animals Under Threat: Great White Shark*. Chicago: Heinemann Library, 2004.

Vogel, Julia and John F. McGee. *Our Wild World: Dolphins*. Chanhassen, Minn.: NorthWord Press, 2001.

Wexo, John Bonnett. *Zoobooks Series: Seals & Sea Lions*. Poway, Calif.: Wildlife Education, 2001.

Index